Karezza

*In memory of
Alice Bunker Stockham (1833-1912),
an outstanding woman,
gynecologist, and social reformer*

Alice B. Stockham

Karezza
Ethics of Marriage

Edited by Heinz Schott
with an Epilogue by the editor

BoD – Books on Demand

Bibliografische Information der Deutschen Nationalbibliothek:

Die Deutsche Nationalbibliothek verzeichnet diese Publikation
in der Deutschen Nationalbibliografie; detaillierte bibliografische
Daten sind im Internet über www.dnb.de abrufbar.

Reprint of the second edition: Chicago 1903
(First edition: Chicago 1896)

Cover photo:
Cherry blossom in Bonn
(H. Schott, 2016)

SCHOTT's NEUE BIBLIOTHEK / 3

© 2017 Heinz Schott
Herstellung und Verlag: BoD – Books on Demand, Norderstedt.

ISBN: 9783744815086

KAREZZA: TABLE OF CONTENTS

GREETING

The author's work, TOKOLOGY, was written from years of professional experience to meet a demand among inquiring women on subjects that deeply concern the physical life of the wife and mother. In these later years the world of thought has grown and new discoveries have been made in spiritual as well as material science.

In answer to hundreds of letters of inquiry I send out this message - KAREZZA, elucidating a theory of conjugal life, in which there is a love communion between husband and wife from which results a mastery of the physical and complete control of the fecundating power.

In *The Familiar Letter* of TOKOLOGY subjects usually considered delicate innature and difficult to handle are presented indirectly and briefly. In an early edition those interested in a "wiser parentage" are cited to a pamphlet written by a distinguished minister, who therein had given to the world a new and unique theory of controlling propagation. Afterwards to my regret and the disappointment of numerous correspondents it was discovered that the work was out of print.

In later editions of TOKOLOGY, alluding to methods of limiting offspring, the following paragraph occurs: "By some a theory called sedular absorption is advanced. This involves intercourse without culmination. No discharge is allowed. People practicing this method claim the highest possible enjoyment, no loss of vitality, and perfect control of the fecundating power."

Many readers asked for further explanation. It proved that the word *Sedular* is not found in the dictionaries, but as used in this connection means *pertaining to seed,* and is so defined in the glossary of the book.

KAREZZA elucidates the above paragraph; gives a high ideal to parental functions; pleads for justice to the unborn child; teaches that the control of procreation is possible with every husband and wife; gives honor to womanhood, and, most of all, controverts the prevailing ideas of baseness and degradation associated with the sexual nature.

KAREZZA may be considered a supplement of TOKOLOGY, and like that, does not deal with ideals, but with tested theories and practical truths. They have been lived and demonstrated, and are here presented to the reader as living facts.

Men and women must learn the significance of the sexual relation, and its possible influence upon life and character. Copulation is more than a propagative act; it is a blending of body, soul and spirit, ennobling or degrading according to the attitude of the participants. For both husband and wife it has a function in soul development that hitherto has been prevented and perverted by the traditional uncleanness attached to this relation. According to man's edict, nature made but one mistake in the evolution of life, and that is, in the human reproductive organs. Reverse this edict, let the search-light of truth illuminate this subject, and a satisfactory solution of many social problems will be evolved. No part of the body should be under condemnation. The young may be enlightened upon important subjects, while the knowledge of sexual science will open the door for the true marriage.

KAREZZA makes a plea for a better birthright for the child, and aims to lead individuals *to* seek a higher development of themselves through most sacred relations. It presents truths that are attainable, and when the goal of mastery is reached, the ideal marriage will be consummated in united lives, giving a prophecy of generations of desired and welcome offspring.

Karezza,
Ethics of Marriage

CHAPTER I
CREATIVE ENERGY

Let there be light.

Man is a trinity of spirit, soul and body. Spirit is the source or God-life of man from which all proceeds. Soul is spirit in action, and embraces all that is recognized as individual, personal existence. Soul includes the intellect, the emotions and the sensations. It is the thinking, loving, living realm of man. From the Spirit through conscious training one is capable of developing unlimited forces and possibilities. Soul looks within, to the All, for life, knowledge and power which it expresses without, through the physical. As thought precedes action, so nothing can appear or manifest itself in the body that has not been conceived or thought of in the soul. Soul may recognize spirit as a governing principle, or it may look out through the senses for material manifestations, depending upon symbols only for its concept of life.

Voluntarily and consciously man may choose between these two roads, - the spiritual or material. In his philosophy, he may recognize and believe all power and all life is from and of the spirit; or, in his philosophy, he may attribute all development, all growth, all evolution from and through matter.

In the spiritual view, recognizing the Divine principle as an ever present, active energy, as life and intelligence operating through the soul upon matter, one comes to conclusions that make all of life's problems less difficult.

Creative energy, expressing through the sexual nature an instinct to perpetuate life, has its origin in, and is coexistent with life itself. It is the power back of all purposes and plans. It is the self-impelling force that gives the ability to do and perform. It is the origin of all activities of child life. It is the inventive genius and impelling factor of all man's handiwork - the thought force of mechanics and machinery.

Both the macrocosms and microcosms of the universe are expressions of the law of life, instinctively put forth by creative energy. This force operates in the multiplication of atoms, in the drawing the pollen upon the stigma; in the attraction of sperm to germ cells. It is the segregation and aggregation of all molecules of matter, founded on the duality of sex.

The processes of growth and fulfillment of functions are propelled by this omnipresent energy of spirit, which is inherent in, and operative through, all nature. It is back of the physical life of man and other animals, and expresses itself through them. Only when it comes with the strong voice of life demanding perpetuation, is it especially a manifestation of the sex nature - a fulfillment of the law of growth, development and increase. Atoms, cells and plants, are unconscious of this life force, and animals conscious only in a small degree.

Man not only has consciousness of this energy, but through his intelligence is capable of developing greater consciousness of its operation and the law governing it. *He knows that* he *knows,* and in this knowledge lies his superiority over the brutes.

This recognition and knowledge makes it possible for man to train this creative potency in all life's purposes and uses. From the inception of the bud of life to its fructifying stage, he may be the master and maker of conditions. There is no karma for him that is not within his own power to mold and make; no passion to usurp authority, no desire that he may not guide and direct. The perfectness of his nature is evolved through the recognition, direction and appropriation of the creative energy, the occult forces of life.

Sexual science based upon this theory teaches that there are deeper purposes and meanings to the reproductive faculties and functions, than are generally understood and taught.

In the physical union of male and female there may be a soul communion giving not only supreme happiness, but in turn conducing to soul growth and development. There may, also be a purpose and power in this communion, when rightly understood, not less significant than the begetting of children. Creative energy in man is manifold in its manifestations, and can be trained into channels of usefulness.

Consciously it may be utilized in every activity, devising, inventing, constructing. It may be directed to building bodily tissue and permeating every cell with health and vigor.

Sex in nature is universal, progressing from lower to higher manifestations of life. it is more distinctive as male and female.

Sexual instinct or passion is a sure sign of seed germination; it is an indication that life may be perpetuated, and that the entire man or woman is in preparation for the culmination of being. It is not an instinct or power either to be ignored or destroyed. Its perversion means physical and spiritual degeneracy.

Seed production is the goal or highest function of tree or plant, and procreation is the complete or ultimate manifestation of man's life. Reproduction is the fulfillment of Divine law.

In the plant and in the tree the life principle fulfills the law of its being in bearing seed. Its manifestation in man is procreation, reproducing another of its kind.

Passion is the instinct for the preservation of one's kind, the voice and the sign of creative power. The highest mission in the rose life is to produce seeds, but on its way it gives beautiful blossoms and fragrant perfume. It may not always be able to fulfill its highest mission, but it can express creative power on its way to fulfillment - to the production of seeds. Man, too, expresses creative life in many ways besides that of parenthood. He preaches a sermon, writes a book, invents a machine. Woman writes a Battle Hymn of the Republic, or makes a loaf of nutritious bread. In both the least and greatest things of life man gives expression to inherent creative principle.

An artist is a creator. Emerson gives the keynote when he says: "Work your passion up into poetry." So with all things, the life principle demanding fulfillment is the power on its way to accomplishment. When the signs of this creative power come throbbing and pulsating into every fibre, it only shows that one has greater ability to create than ever before. There are varied and definite appropriations for this energy.

Knowledge of the law of the spirit, gives the ability to control this power and all its signs. One becomes its master as truly as is the engineer of his engine, or the electrician who has controlled the most potent force or power known to man. The physical sign appearing as passion is of the spirit and not of the flesh. Treat it as the voice of power impelling one to do, to work. Say quickly, "What new work is before me? I am a creator. What shall I create?" The sign is a proof of strength and ability to do greater things than yet accomplished. Demand of the spiritual self to know what that work may be. Listen, listen to the voice; the intuition or Higher Self in the silence of the soul will give answer.

Then think, plan and work for fulfillment.

Religion and philosophy are required in consecrating passion. One inspires a faith in the source of all power, the other defines man's relation to that power. Already, perhaps, the heart-life is devoted to some great work, some mission to humanity, but now include directly and specifically in this consecration creative energy, the inherent impelling, burgeoning force of life. This inherent force is so prominent in its demands, so ever-present in action and intrinsically so allied to cosmic force, that it deserves and requires a special consecration. It must be known as good and not evil, as a friend and not an enemy, as a quickening, generating power. Consciously, thoughtfully and specifically command its service. In no way does man's dominion yield him a richer return than in control, mastery and consecration of sex energy. It is a means to achievement in any definite direction. The marvel is that as consciousness of internal strength and power develops, the physical sign disappears. The peace that follows is the peace of power.

Understanding the law, that all naturally and inherently is good, no base or ignoble thoughts of the reproductive functions can ever enter the mind. The growth, development and ripening of the human seed, becomes a sweet and sacred mystery, and may be studied as a science with the same pleasure, the same purity of thought, with which one studies plant life and all its revelations.

12

One finds that nature has no secrets that need be withheld. A striking analogy is seen in the seed cradled in the pod, the birdling in its nest, and the incipient human life lovingly protected in the mother's organism. By this pure ideal a profound reverence for all of nature's mysteries and unfathomable secrets is developed; a conservation of energies is accomplished; while through the baptizing consecration of thought, the generative organs are redeemed from the desecration of the past, and their powers and functions justly and wisely appropriated.

This conservation of power is both possible and effective for the unmarried. Through love, training and self-control, however, the married may not only attain the same conservation and appropriation but also by the union of the spiritual forces of their two souls, greatly augment them.

Love is the fulfillment of the law. Sexual love is its highest expression on the earth- plane, and sexual union is symbolical of this love. It stands as evidence of creative energy in action. Love is the impelling power, and as through affinity and attraction, a chemical union takes place between two substances producing other substances, so in a union of the sexes on the spiritual plane, accomplishes results greater than could be accomplished separately. The artist has visions of new creations, the author has inspirations for new works, the inventor has new plans and models for machinery and devices. There is no limit to the power of a true soul union. It specifically increases the gift of healing and may be purposely directed to free a friend from pain and suffering.

The sexual union which is planned and controlled, becomes glorified through conscious appropriation, while new meanings and new powers are given to conjugal love. This conservation, furthermore, is a precursor and preparation for parenthood; for the conception of welcome and desired offspring that shall in turn have the inheritance of loving intention and premeditated wisdom.

As the creative potency of man becomes understood, and as this knowledge is applied, men and women will grow in virtue, in love, in power, and will gladly and naturally devote this power to the world's interests and development.

CHAPTER II
KAREZZA

Whatsoever things are true, whatsoever things are honest, whatsoever things are just, whatsoever things are pure, whatsoever things are lovely, whatsoever things are of good report; if there be any virtue and if there be any praise, think on these things.

Karezza signifies "to express affection in both words and actions," and while it fittingly denotes the union that is the outcome of deepest human affection, love's consummation, it is used technically throughout this work to designate a controlled sexual relation.

Intelligent married people, possessing lofty aims in life and desiring spiritual growth and development, have it in their power so to accord their marital relations as to give an untold impetus to all their faculties. This is given through the act of copulation when it is the outgrowth of the expressions of love, and is at the same time completely under the control of the will

The ordinary hasty spasmodic method of cohabitation, for which there has been no previous preparation, and in which the wife is passive is alike unsatisfactory to husband and wife. It is deleterious both physically and spiritually. It has in it no consistency as a demonstration of affection, and is frequently a cause of estrangement and separation.

Karezza so consummates marriage that through the power of will, and loving thoughts, the crisis is not reached, but a complete control by both husband and wife is maintained throughout the entire relation.

The law of Karezza dictates thoughtful preparation, even for several days previous to the union. Lover-like attentions and kindly acts prophesy love's appointed consummation. These bind heart to heart and soul to soul. There should be a course of training to exalt the spiritual and subordinate the physical. This is accomplished through reading and meditation. The reading should lead to exaltation of spirit, and to the knowledge of the power and source of life.

The authors chosen should be illuminated souls, such as Browning,

Emerson, Carpenter. It is not easy to advise for individual cases. W.F. Evans, Henry Wood, and R.W. Trine have revealed the law of spirit and given practical helps in life's adjustment.

The meditation should be an act of giving up of one's will, one's intellectual concepts, to allow free usurpation of cosmic intelligence. In obedience to law, common or finite consciousness listens to cosmic consciousness. Daily, hourly, the listening soul awakens to new ideals.

At the pointed time, without fatigue of body or unrest of mind, accompany general bodily contact with expressions of endearment and affection, followed by the complete but quiet union of the sexual organs. During a lengthy period of perfect control, the whole being of each is submerged into the other, and an exquisite exaltation experienced. This may be followed by a quiet motion, entirely under subordination of the will, so that the thrill of passion for either may not go beyond a pleasurable exchange. Unless procreation is desired, let the final propagative orgasm be entirely avoided.

With abundant time and mutual reciprocity, the interchange becomes satisfactory and complete without emission or crisis. In the course of an hour the physical tension subsides, the spiritual exaltation increases, and not uncommonly visions of a transcendent life are seen and consciousness of new powers experienced.

Before and during the time there may be some devotional exercises or there may be a formula of consecration of an uplifting character in which both unite. This aids in concentration and in removing the thoughts from merely physical sensations. The fol- lowing phrase has been helpful to many: "We are living spiritual beings; our bodies symbolize soul union, and in closest contact each receives strength to be more to each other and more to all the world."

This method of consummating the marriage relation is erroneously called in TOKOLOGY, Sedular Absorption. Many scientists now believe there is no seed fluid secreted except through the demand of the final act of expulsion. If this be true, in Karezza there is no seed to be absorbed, as, under the direct control of the will, the act ceases short of the seed secreting period.

One writer called it Male Continence, but it is no more male than female continence; to secure the greatest good, the husband and wife equally conserve their forces under a wise control; besides, Continence has long been erroneously accepted as the term for abstinence of the physical relation except for procreation.

Karezza is a symbol of the perfect union of two souls in marriage, it is the highest expression of mutual affection, and gives to those practicing it revelations of strength and power. It must be experienced upon a higher plane than the merely physical, and may always be made a means of spiritual unfoldment. This should be called a spiritual rather than a physical companionship. With a due reverence for the deeper meanings of the association, union and soul development are sought rather than fleeting passional gratification.

Karezza gives to the sexual relation an office entirely distinct from the propagative act, a high office in individual development and formation of character. It is both a union on the affectional plane and a preparation for best possible conditions for procreation.

Karezza should always be the outcome, the emblem of the deeper emotions; both husband and wife should hope and expect that the union will contribute to their spiritual growth and development. The marriage bond has given the sex functions a special consecration. In each union under spiritual law this consecration is renewed. There is no defilement or debasement in the natural and controlled expression of sexual love.

Karezza does not lead to asceticism or repression, but rather to appropriation and expression. In acknowledging the life source and conscientiously devoting the creative principle to achievement, to the activities and purposes of life, one is put in possession of new powers and possibilities.

The time and frequency Karezza can be governed by no certain law. Experience, however, has proven that it is far more satisfactory to have at least an interval of two to four weeks, and many find that even three or four months afford greater impetus to power and growth as well as more personal satisfaction; during the interval the thousand and one lover-like attentions give reciprocal delight, and are an anticipating prophecy of the ultimate union.

According to the law of Karezza, *the demand for physical expression is less frequent,* for there is a deep soul union that is replete with satisfaction and is lasting. As a symbol it embodies all the manifestations of conjugal love. In all departments of life symbols be- come less necessary as one develops spiritually. So in this relation one may possibly outgrow the symbol. But both growth and satisfaction are attained through altruistic desires, and through the mutual recognition and response by husband and wife to the innermost nature of each - the higher self.

Be patient and determined; the reward will come in happy united lives, in the finding of the kingdom of heaven in your own hearts through obedience to law.

Spencer truly said: "When any law works to the advantage of the human race, then hu- man nature infallibly submits to it, since obedience to it becomes a pleasure to man." Yes, the pleasure is in obedience, for all our sufferings come from ignorance of the law of being, and failure of adjustment to that law.

Men and women should be as willing to learn the law of sex expression as they are to study any other science of life, or any law of nature. It should not only be an intellectual study, but should be a study of experience and adjustment. In *Karezza* this expression and adjustment are so largely personal that special rules cannot be given, but those seeking the highest development will soon establish conditions.

CHAPTER III

ATTAINMENT POSSIBLE

It is the spirit that quickeneth;
the flesh profiteth nothing.

No doubt if the ideas herein presented are new, the first thought will be that it is impossible, that no one can so regulate his life as thus proposed. But scores of married men and women attest that such self-control as Karezza requires is perfectly possible.

At all times to subordinate the physical senses and desires to the spiritual is a matter of education and growth in the knowledge of the laws of being - a knowledge of the power of the spiritual nature.

There is no part of the body that is not under the dominion of the mind, and that cannot be influenced by an intelligent voluntary mental action. Certain physiological processes and muscular movements that ordinarily have been classed involuntary are really carried on by an unconscious or sub- conscious action of the mind, by the intelligent operation of creative energy.

The body of itself cannot think, cannot move, cannot perpetuate itself. It is made up of solids, fluids and gases, and without mind, it has no power; it has no living, moving, breathing, creating force in itself.

Creative energy as intelligence enables us to breathe, day in and day out, sleeping or waking. Mind in its unerring and subconscious action propels the heart's blood through radiating channels and microscopic tubes, defying the law of gravitation and keeping a uniform rhythm day and night for scores of years.

It is mind, surely, that enables cells to discriminate and take from heterogeneous varieties of food, and appropriate with an orderly and unerring skill, material for either bone, muscle or sinew.

All physiological functions and vital processes can be modified by a conscious action of the intellect, a voluntary mental effort. This is true of the liver, the kidneys, the skin and the processes of digestion, circulation, excretion and secretion. They are not automatic and fixed beyond our control as has been taught.

One breathes naturally about twenty times a minute, but by a very little effort one may train the subconscious mind, so unceasingly engaged in inspiration and expiration, to hold the breath for a long period of time.

Although one winks unconsciously when an object flits suddenly before the vision, still consciously, he can steadily hold the eye open and gaze at the same object.

Darwin mentions the case of a person who could suspend the pulsations of the heart at pleasure, and of another who could move his bowels at will - accelerating their peristaltic action by thought alone.

Thinking of fruit, sour or luscious, affects the salivary glands and causes the mouth to water. The thought of some stimulant or medicinal preparation has an effect similar to that of the thing itself, even if less in degree.

Many years since I had a patient to whom I had given a preparation of podophyllum[1] for a torpid liver. Two or three powders produced the desired result.

Several months afterwards he laughingly told me that he had carried one of those powders in his pocket, and whenever he thought he needed to stimulate the action of the liver, he imagined the taste and peculiar properties of the remedy, and soon was happy in having the desired result although he still preserved the powder. This was at least a more economical procedure for the patient than for the doctor.

Medical science is coming to recognize the power of thought over all bodily functions, and it is possible that the laws of the mind will become so universally understood, that desired action of special functions can be obtained without even carrying the remedy in the pocket.

All so-called physical sensations represent conditions of thought, or rather results and effects of thought building, and are more or less under control of the mind's action.

Habits of thought produce and govern susceptibility to degrees of temperature, to barometric conditions; to varied effects of food and drink.

For one, sensation, lays down the law of heat and cold to the nicety of a degree, while for another through certain rheumatic pains or stings, it predicts a westerly gale or a northeastern thunderstorm. Is it any glory to make thermometers and barometers of our bodies through our cultivated sensations? Will it not rather redound to one's credit if he has power of adaptation, and has ceased to limit his activities through his feelings??

The body, which has been coddled and babied through the centuries, is not the living man and must not dominate him. *Man is a living, spiritu-*

---

[1] herbs

al being. Recognition and acknowledgement of the power of the spirit, not only frees him from limitation of the senses, but gives him dominion over every faculty and function of the body.

"It is the glory of man to control himself," and the best use to make of his life is to develop and demonstrate the supremacy of the spiritual over the physical.

Only within a few years have Western people learned that they can consciously and systematically train all their powers. This training enables the possessor to attain health, strength, peace of mind and control of the body.

Karezza teaches the supreme action of the will over the sexual nature, as well as the complete appropriation of the creative energy to high aims, lofty purposes and enduring results. In this knowledge man is no more the machine to be buffeted by circumstance and environment; he is rather the machinist having control of both the mechanism and the power of the bodily instrument. He recognizes in his spiritual nature the *real man* which has unlimited resources, and he claims the ability to remove self-made limitations. He enthrones his divine nature which gives dominion and mastery, and at no time does this dominion serve him with more satis- faction than in the marital relation of husband and wife, thus making possible the attainment of Karezza.

CHAPTER IV

HEALTH

All life in nature is perfect; man's life is no exception
if he removes self-made limitations.

Karezza is strengthening and sustaining to husband and wife, because it is virtually a union of the higher selves, from which naturally there can be no reaction. As the spiritual is developed, the physical is subordinated. Whatever contributes to soul growth enhances the power to live free from the domination of the body, and bodily sensations. Thus is secures

20

harmonious physical conditions, and the spirit manifests or pictures itself through the flesh as a harmonious whole.

Especially is it necessary for the wife to be freed from the usual dread of excessive and undesired child- bearing. Fear and anxious thought, far more than bacilli or bacteria, are productive of pain, disease and suffering. The terrors and dread of childbirth, the horrors of undesired maternity, have been potent factors in causing the weakness and the suffering of women.

To know that childbirth is natural, and that under harmonious conditions it is not attended by suffering, removes a great curse from the lives of women. To know that the inherent desire for maternity is to be fulfilled under the best conditions and entirely at her own command, is a wonderful boon to woman.

If, on the other hand, women are resigned to conditions that they deem unavoidable, and patiently pay in frequent childbirths what they consider the penalty of their sex, they become little more than breeding animals. They are given no time for self-development and preparation for their obligations to the fast increasing family.

Instances are rare when women can maintain a high standard of health and strength and bear six or eight children in ten or twelve years, and at the same time perform the combined offices of nurse, cook, laundress, seamstress and governess. In drudgery they drag along through days and nights, with no outlook for the future save a recurrence of similar conditions.

Every woman owes it to herself to preserve the normal elasticity of health and strength, to become enduring for all the many obligations and activities of life, so to accord all her thinking and living that increase of years will not be attended by weakness and debility. Her maturer years, on the contrary, should be filled with increasing strength and power, veritably with the health and buoyancy of youth. The young "old lady" should become the regenerated "new woman," the glory and inspiration of the coming time. This may be consummated through the aid of Karezza

In Karezza the husband also experiences conditions which preserve his health and natural, vital powers.

Physicists have demonstrated with incontrovertible facts that it is eminently healthy to conserve the virile principle. The seminal secretion has a wonderful imminent value, and if retained is absorbed into the system and adds enormously to a man's magnetic, mental and spiritual force. In ordinary married life this force is constantly being wasted. Other things being equal, the man who wisely conserves is in concentrated mental and physical power and effectiveness, like a Daniel and his companions. He builds and constructs, he is the orator and the inventor. He is the leader of great movements, because his power is drawn from an inexhaustible storage battery

The testes may be considered analogous to the salivary and lachrymal glands, in which there is no fluid secreted except at the demand of their respective functions. The thought of food makes the mouth water for a short time only, while the presence of the food causes an abundant yield of saliva.

It is customary for physiologists to assume that the spermatic secretion is analogous to bile, which when once formed, must be expelled.

But substitute the word tears for bile, and you put before the mind an idea altogether different. Tears, as falling drops, are not essential to life and health. A man may be in perfect health and not cry once in five or even fifty years. The lachrymal fluid is ever present, but in such small quantities that it is unnoticed. Where are tears while they remain unshed? They are ever ready, waiting to spring forth when there is an adequate cause, but they do not accumulate and distress the man because they are not shed daily, weekly or monthly. The component elements of the tears are prepared in the system, they are on hand, passing through the circulation, ready to mix and flow whenever they are needed; but if they mix, accumulate and flow without adequate cause, there is a disease of the lachrymal glands. While there are no exact analogues in the body, yet the tears and the spermatic fluids are much more analogous in their normal manner of secretion and use than are the bile and the semen. Neither flow of tears nor of semen is essential to life or health. Both are largely under the control of the imagination, the emotions, and the will; and the flow of either is liable to be arrested in a moment by sudden mental action.

It is as degrading for them to allow a seminal emission without rational and proper cause, as it is unmanly for them to shed tears frequently or on trivial occasions. If they could know, moreover, that an uncalled for emission is a destructive waste of life material, perhaps the formation of habits of masturbation, promiscuous intercourse and marital profligacy, with all their disastrous consequences, might be largely prevented.

The mammary gland is an apt illustration of the law of demand and supply. In its anatomical construction and physiological function is it not analogous to the producing gland of the male?

No one has ever hinted that it is essential for health that the natural lacteal fluid of the mammary gland must be continually or frequently secreted and expelled. It is not considered a "physical necessity" or a demand of nature. Indeed, the contrary opinion prevails, that an abundant flow of milk may be derogative to healthful conditions.

Milk flows in answer to the demand of a newborn infant, and should it come at any other time than when thus demanded, it is considered a perversion of nature and an unnecessary drain upon the system. May it not prove that the unnecessary secretion and expulsion of the semen is as great a perversion of nature?

May it not also prove that erectile tissue in action is not a positive evidence of secretion in the gland?

Physiology alone proves that the practice of Karezza imparts health and strength to man. When it is known that conservation is not so much the result of retained secretions as the transmutation and transformation of vital forces, - the innermost life of man, then students will cease testing the fluids with chemicals, and the bodily tissue with microscope and scalpel.

Although woman has not the semen to conserve, yet equally with man she has the thrilling potency of passion, that when well directed, heals sensitive nerves, vitalizes the blood and restores tissue. In this deeper, truer union, the very heart of Karezza, woman as well as man prevents and cures disease. Karezza has a therapeutic value not equaled by any remedy of pharmacopia, or by any system of healing.

The natural woman knows that virtue is not sexual repression but rather expression; that coldness, inertness, and want of feeling are due to condemnation of the life that is the center and creator of all life. She has been taught shame for the most sacred relations, and especially for the sign of the power that creates offspring, but she reverses this teaching. Is a plant ashamed to bud, bloom and bring forth fruit?

Women must bless the source of life; she must be loyal to her trust. She must know that sex life and sex expression are a natural heritage, God implanted.

Wisely, thoughtfully should she seek conservation and appropriation of that which is the heart of vitality.

Men who are borne down with sorrow because their wives are nervous, feeble and irritable, have it in their own power, through Karezza,, to restore the radiant hue of health to the faces of their loved ones, strength and elasticity to their steps and harmonious action of every part of their bodies. By manifestation of tenderness and endearment, the husband may develop a response in the wife through her love nature, which thrills every fiber into action and radiates tonic to every nerve.

Men with hearts full of love and wisdom will not be slow to accord this boon to wives whom they have pledged to love and protect, thus fulfilling the marriage sacrament.

In Karezza, creative energy is transmuted into the very life of the cell, from which is developed perfect structure and tissue. The impetus to health derived from Karezza is the right of every man and woman. It is co-operative building, love being the foundation, wisdom the designer and executor. This planning and building prophesy perpetual youth, and progeny surpassing all progenitors in strength and endurance.

CHAPTER V
PARENTHOOD

The desire for fatherhood and motherhood, is found and expressed in the sexual instinct which in turn evinces and is the sign of creative power. Its origin is in life itself. It is the God power in us, and when it comes throbbing and pulsating in every nerve, in every thought and feeling, it should be recognized as such and appropriated in a God-like manner.

The power to perpetuate the life principle is from the spiritual side of life. It is a manifestation of spirit in the flesh. Body alone cannot reproduce itself, the physical man cannot perpetuate himself, the physical woman cannot perpetuate herself.

Reproduction is from and through spiritual life. It is creative energy manifested in flesh. Its fulfillment is in parenthood.

Parenthood being an expression of creative principle, and being born of the spirit, need not necessarily have its sole manifestation in the procreation of children in the flesh. It can be devoted to, and expressed in, all the great interests of the world.

The inventing, creating, organizing and systematizing qualities of the male; the patience, the carefulness, tenderness and attention to details, indeed, the brooding care of the female - all these are greatly needed in our government, in our religious and educational institutions, in all the affairs of life.

The human craving of either father or mother, may find expression in the larger, greater and all-inclusive power of Divine love, in its devotion to some great philanthropy, or in its concentration upon some altruistic work.

Parenthood, recognized as a manifestation of the Divine in man, as the highest and noblest expression of manhood and woman- hood, gives a choice of appropriation either to spiritual or physical procreation. In Karezza this choice is under certain and wise control.

The desire for offspring is innate in the human heart; it is the natural expression of the creative principle; it is seed-bearing on the physical plane.

In my professional experience more women have consulted me to ascertain and overcome causes of barrenness, than have sought to prevent motherhood. Those denied the privileges and blessings of maternity usually have been borne down with a great sorrow. Very few have yet learned that this maternal desire may be gratified on a higher plane through the procreation of thought and ideas, and thus give satisfaction to a natural instinct.

Physiology and pathology alike often fail to reveal the causes of barrenness, while the physician's resources and the surgeon's knife alike afford no relief. Very frequently the cause lies deeper than can be discovered by chemistry and the microscope, or remedied by probe and scalpel. The cause may lie in the occult forces, in the lack of soul or spiritual adjustment, or it may have its origin in physical excesses.

Conservation is the great secret of power. It is possible that the heart's desire for offspring may be gratified through *Karezza*, through wise and temperate control of the sexual impulses, a storage of life that begets life.

In Karezza men and women attain such development and fine spiritual perception that they know when a soul can be begotten, and will to the great power resulting from continence quickly respond.

Many cases of sterility have been overcome even by an occasional and unsystematic temperance in the physical relation. A fruitful union frequently follows long separation of husband and wife, even though they have never had children. One may expect more certain results if the relation conforms to scientific principles.[2]

---

[2] Since penning the above a lady called, aged 39, who had been married thirteen years, without children. At last, however, her mother heart throbbed with happy anticipations. In conversation the fact was developed that conception had taken place immediately after a lengthy separation from her husband. Seed waste was prevented and propagation was the result. Through Karezza this seed waste can be prevented without separation, and thus the heart's longing for children be gratified.

CHAPTER VI
CONTROL OF PROCREATIVE POWERS

No words can express the helplessness, the sense of personal desecration, the despair which sinks into the heart of a woman forced to submit to maternity under adverse circumstances, and when her own soul rejects it. - H. C. Wright.

Through Karezza unsought and undesired paternity will be a thing of the past. Children that are desired will be planned for, favorable conditions will be sought, and the conception of a human being will be an occa- sion for the highest expression of creative power.

Time, circumstances and conditions for the best good of the parent and the child may be chosen.

The control of the fecundating power appeals especially to those mothers who are forced into frequent childbearing, who not only suffer in loss of health and strength themselves, but are overwhelmed by their inability to do justice to their children. If such mothers are rich, the little ones are turned to the pitiless care of a nurse; if poor, the children must seek their own diversion and all their activities thus lack wise direction. Alas! They are physical mothers only, lacking the unperverted and unerring maternal instinct of the lower creation.

Women instinctively long for and desire the office of motherhood. With this desire it is natural that they should wish suitable conditions and circumstances to enable them to perform the office well, to give children a rightful inheritance and to have the sacred office honored. It is lack of these conditions for maternity that impels women to shrink from it.

Fear of suffering also, that frequently attends the office, causes women to dread motherhood, and often has led them to use undue measures to prevent it; it is now known that suffering is not a natural consequence of child-bearing. Even on the physical plane if women live close to the heart of nature, adopting simple habits of dress, food and exercise, they can to a great degree prevent the pangs of childbirth. It has been proven over and over again that *painless parturition is possible.*

A great truth, however, has been discovered. Through a knowledge of the spiritual forces of life and the possibility of according one's life to the law governing them, one may, under all circumstances, experience health and harmony. The inference follows that the natural functions of pregnancy and parturition, aided by a knowledge of this truth, will be free from pain and disability.

The very desire to realize the spiritual ideal in reproduction, together with consecration of the reproductive functions to that ideal, tends of itself to lessen suffering.

The very young should be trained in this ideal. Girls, as children, should early have instilled into their minds reverence for all the functions in their natures pertaining to the maternal. At the approach of womanhood, a sign of the development and ripening of the ovules occurs in what is called menstruation. Girls should be taught that this is a symbol of motherhood, a sign that the ovules are being prepared for the fructifying principle. They have already learned that the ovule of flowers is found embedded in a cell to which pollen is carried from the anthers through the stigma. Thus seed germination is accomplished.

Speaking plainly, it is the sexual intercourse of plant life, from which baby plants are produced.

There is such a close analogy sexually between human and plant life that it should be taught with the same freedom and reverence. Most emphatically the young should never receive the idea of shame or debasement in connection with any natural function.

A girl should know that the highest goal of her life is reproduction. All signs pointing to this should be joyfully welcomed. The indications of womanhood are a pledge of motherhood. The inherent maternal instinct has been expressed in fondness for dolls, foreshadowing the joys of maternity; she gladly learns that maturity gives her the possibility of its fulfillment.

Women must understand that childbearing is a natural expression of creative energy. They and their physicians have looked upon and treated the function as a disease, and ignorantly coddled and encouraged the disorders attending it. Maternity is a divinely appointed mission, - to be a mother is a sacred trust. To reverence this trust and to come into close communion with the heart of all life replaces fear and dread with joy and satisfaction. This is an agreement with nature's plan, a law of spirit. Acknowledgement of and obedience to this law lessen or entirely overcome the usual sufferings of pregnancy and parturition.

Fearing nothing, but hoping and expecting the greatest earthly felicity, women will cease to dread or to prevent childbearing on account of the dangers attending it, for through knowledge there is nothing to fear.

For the sake, however, of the best conditions for the development and birth of the child, men and women should intelligently and consciously control the fecundating power. Every child has a right to a parent- age of thoughtful preparation, to the best that can be given him. In Karezza this right of the unborn child is fulfilled. He becomes the inheritor of love's behests and wise designs, which shape and mold his entire life and character.

It has been taught that to fulfill literally the command to "multiply and replenish" means that it is God's law to submit to chance conception. Under other similar circumstances, that which would be called an accident or incident, is in the procreation of a human being called a special providence.

In his undeveloped wisdom man may provide protection and education for his child, but fail to seek an opportunity for that child's conception, at a time when its protection and education can be assured.

Man takes circumstances into his own hands and accumulates a fortune for the child to inherit, but he does not give a thought to the conditions that bequeath to that child health and wisdom to enjoy and appropriate such an inheritance.

Men and women devote their best years to education and culture, to discoveries of ethnology in language, history and art, to the interpretation of Norse legends and Oriental myths, to the deepest philosophical and metaphysical questions, but in all this learning and wisdom not one thought is ever breathed that will give to a child an inheritance of thoughtful preparation, and chosen conditions.

Men inaugurate kindergartens, schools and colleges for post-natal training, but in no wise do they institute plans and preparations for any pre-natal culture.

This lack of knowledge and instruction directly deprives children of the best birth- right, and is nowise consistent with the many other measures inaugurated for the protection and development of human beings. We should accord to every child the great privilege of a birth that affords the best advantage possible, and to do this the time and occasion should be chosen for the purpose.

Karezza affords a certain scientific method of controlling procreation, one in which there can be no objection on account of health, and one that appeals to the reason of every think- ing person.

Under wise control unwelcome children will be unknown, and the brand of selfish desires and indulgence will no longer be impressed upon the infant mind. As future generations understand the law of spiritual growth and mastery, their children will be superior in power and achievement to any heretofore known.

Why should we not accord to a human being even greater intelligence in its parenthood, its inception and development, than is given to the propagation of animals?

Have we no intelligent protest against the ordinary chance procreation? Will not love, science and wisdom, combined with prophetic intelligence for the betterment of the race, devise and promulgate a theory of scientific reproduction?

Oh men of science and wisdom, open your storehouses of knowledge, and pour it forth to supply this demand! Oh women with hearts full of love and intuition! Can you not tenderly lead your sisters to understand a wise and benign appropriation of their creative powers in which the welfare of offspring shall have first consideration?

Shall not the world cease to be peopled by unloved and undesired children? Let love be the fulfillment of law, and let us have a race of men and women that will bless the wisdom, consideration and deliberation of their progenitors.

Breathe the spirit of progress into the institution of marriage and let all strive for descendants that shall glorify the centuries to come. Through thought force creative energy should project itself forward in time, and give our children's children a birthright of love and an inheritance more priceless than precious stones. Let us multiply the Emersons, the Savonarolas, the Catherines of Siena, for they in turn will bless the earth.

CHAPTER VII
FREE MOTHERHOOD

A partnership with God is motherhood.
What strength, what purity, what self-control,
What love, what wisdom belongs to her.
Who helps God fashion an immortal soul.
-Mary Wood Allen.

When in India I visited the Naiars, a peculiar people, found on the Malabar Coast, and claiming to be of Brahmin descent. They have a native government, are intelligent and educated, have good schools and their houses average better than those in other parts of India.

Except two sisters who conducted a mission industrial school for girls, there were no English in this Province. The great peculiarity of the Naiars is that the women are the *lords of creation.* In wide contrast to the condition of other women of that country so full of inconsistencies, they are called the *free women* of India.

They seek their husbands, control business interests, and through them only is the descent of property.

The family and the whole fabric of society is founded upon *the mother.* She is the keystone of the arch, for she chooses who shall be the father of her child and bestows her worldly goods according to her desires and discretion.

She marries the man of her choice. If for any reason, however, she deems him unfit to be a husband or a father of her child, it requires no ceremony of church or state to free her from him. Her wish and word are law.

Karezza gives a free motherhood, whether in a government controlled by men or women. Karezza is a mutual relation and it removes all vestiges of the old idea of man's dominion over the woman. All the pleasure and benefits to be derived are hers as much as his.

The institution of marriage becomes ideal when the desire and pleasure of the wife calls forth the desire and pleasure of the husband - when a single code of ethics governs their relation. When offspring is desired, then surely it is for woman to command and man to obey.

Henry C. Wright, a noble defender of the rights of women and children, said: "Man, in begetting a child without regard to the wishes and condition of his wife, heedless of the physical and spiritual well being of his offspring, commits the greatest outrage any human being can perpetrate on another. Motherhood should be a privilege and an opportunity, not a penalty or misfortune."

When all people concede the importance and dignity of the maternal function, then all will honor and respect woman as does Drummond in his *Ascent of Man.* He maintains that "Mothers are the chief end of creation. In plants the mother species heads the list. Beyond the mother with her milky breast the Creator does not go; that is His goal. In as real a sense as a factory is meant to turn out locomotives or locks, the machinery of nature in its last resort is meant to turn out mothers."

In these and various eloquent paragraphs this man of science honors motherhood. He exclaims that love is the supreme factor in the evolution of the world, and teaches that the mother in giving birth to children, in caring for them and educating them, gives us the highest manifestation of Divine love.

We reverence the high ideals of this philosopher, and esteem him for his fearlessness. Those, however, who have studied deeply into spiritual truth, do not recognize great mental and spiritual differences between men and women on account of sex.

Circumstances and environments have made seeming differences. The best development and the purest lives come from a full understanding and recognition of the purely spiritual or divine in man. The knowledge of the living, spiritual truth that man has no separate existence from God, is the most potent factor in breaking down all supposed inequalities between the sexes. This gives us a new language. There is no more talk of male or female minds, male or female qualities, for all minds are from one source. Each individual includes in his characteristics both male and female principles, both the fatherhood and motherhood of God.

When we come to know that the larger experience is in the spiritual life, neither man nor woman will patter around in Chinese shoes of conventionalism, or have their conduct governed by conditions as binding as Hindu Caste.

This gives to woman freedom with its basic principles in spiritual law. She realizes that the source of love, wisdom and knowledge is infinite, that life in its fullness is hers; that the possibilities of conquest are as great as the world, and the path is as free and wide as the universe.

She finds her true self in every situation.

She loses even a suspicion that anyone wishes or has the power to curtail her privileges, while her daily external life becomes a manifestation of her internal growth and exaltation.

The mother-nature demanding the divinest helps, in the existence of the demand feels the assurance of the supply. In the desire and fulfillment of the office of maternity, her choice as to time and circumstances becomes law.

Women have demanded and received recognition in every profession and vocation; they have eloquently appealed for the duties and privileges of citizenship. In many states they have been allowed through the ballot, a voice in adjusting disputed policies of city and country; they have been given positions of responsibility and emolument; but alas, how seldom are they accorded the freedom of choice for the fulfillment of the inherent and natural function of child- bearing.

Elizabeth Cady Stanton, after thirty years devotion to the enfranchisement of woman, said that if the ballot were granted fully and freely to women, she would have entered only the vestibule to her emancipation; and that with the conditions that love and freedom would give to her sexual life she could raise a race of gods.

Women in every station of life, from the reigning queen of the greatest nation of the earth to the humblest toiler in the hamlet; wives of men expounding the higher law from the pulpit and wives of men in slums, ignorant of all law and justice, have all alike, been subjected to all the inconvenience, suf- fering and debasement of chance maternity. Thus the hearts of intelligent and pure-minded people have been dulled by tradition to the injustice and wrong thus perpetrated upon both mother and child.

Women whose intuitions have been trained to lofty purposes and aims will seek and expect best conditions for procreation. The child in its glorified life will bless her thoughtfulness and fidelity. In freedom the behests of love are fulfilled. Ideal parentage gives ideal children.

It belongs to institutions of learning to remove from sexual science the stigma of secrecy and prudery, and it is the privilege of enlightened womanhood to apply scientific knowledge to the conception and bearing of children; to apply the accumulated wisdom of the ages to the most responsible office of maternity. To do this she must be free to exalt her sexual life to the fulfillment of its highest mission. In this enlightenment and exaltation, the devoted husband will naturally and freely accord his conduct to her wishes. Love's commands are always founded on justice; love's obedience is willing obedience.

Happy he with such a mother! Faith in womankind
Beats with his blood, and trust in all things high
comes easy to him.

CHAPTER VIII
MARRIED AND MATED

It is the woman of you and not the physical body which is the wife. Nature is a system of nuptials. All exist as the offspring or product of a marriage.
- Grindon.

Karezza develops a closer bond of union between husband and wife. They two are united for life; they enter the marriage relation thoughtfully with the hope of happiness and mutual helpfulness. But what a travesty is the usual marriage upon the one idealized, not only in song and story, but in every loving heart. How soon many hearts are broken and many hopes blasted, and mainly because the sexual relationship in marriage is instigated by selfish motives, and for personal gratification.

Marriage is a man-made institution to protect nature in her plan - to surround and guard individuals with restraint for the benefit of the community. Marriage is the one morally conceded and legally recognized form of association of one man with one woman, granting the rights and privileges of the sexual relation as husband and wife.

Men and women begin married life without a true estimate of the relation to be sustained. They do not realize that all conduct of life in its bearings and results, depends upon a law, a law deeper in its fundamental principles and more nearly just in its execution, than any human law. Marital unhappiness is chiefly caused by ignorance of the psycho- physiological laws governing the relations between the sexes, and ignorance of what is due to each from the other in all of their associations, more especially in the sexual union.

In ignorance, every couple enters marriage as a new experience. At present there is no education except that of observation, and no school except that of experience, to fit people for living together in marriage. They enter the relation believing it to be for life; for better and not for worse. The young and inexperienced enter it tempted by love, full of energy, desire and expectation; others, more mature in years, through a wider knowledge of the ways of the world, for reasons, perhaps, better considered and weighed.

With few exceptions the subjects of procreation, pregnancy and all matters pertaining to sexual science, are tabooed between the sexes previous to marriage. By the "holy bans" of the priest, the Gordian knot of secrecy is loosened. The shrinking timidity of the wife is met by a bravado of superior knowledge of the husband. He is imbued with the belief - an iron-clad tradition of the ages - that marriage gives him a special license.

Under this license often and often he puts to shame the prostitution of the brothel. Too frequently, alas, the sweet flower of love is blighted forever.

The day of wedding bells, of blooming exotics and friendly congratulations, ends in a night of suffering and sorrow. The love must be strong and deep that can withstand selfish gratification, especially if the gratification be for one only at the expense, pain and disappointment of the other.

Lift the veil of secrecy from these subjects, and study sexual science with greater care and devotion than you give to furnishing the cottage in which you expect to live. No better thing can be done to cement lives in the promised union and to insure the hoped for happiness.

True marriage is based upon that recognition of the individuality of both husband and wife which brings voluntary, not compelled, co-operation in all the departments of family life. Only when souls, flowing together, acting as one, distinct in individuality, but united in their action are thus mated, are the psycho-- physiological laws met and satisfied.

"Whosoever looketh on a woman to lust after her hath committed adultery." Tolstoi says: "These words relate not only to the wife of another, but especially to one's own wife. Woman in bringing a child into the world, and giving it her bosom, sees clearly that her affairs are more serious than those of man.

Consequently woman is necessarily superior to man. She becomes superior by the acts of generation, birth, and nursing."

Painful recitals of unwritten annals of the lives of those who endure in silence or seek relief through the courts from wrongs inflicted, would fill volumes. Better knowledge of the relations between husband and wife would avoid these conditions. There are earnest, intelligent people today who have come to believe that marriage should and can be lifted to a plane of spiritual companionship far exceeding any pleasure known to the merely physical.

There can be no marriage unless attraction, affinity and harmony first exist in the soul. True union, indeed, depends on a psychic law; and its permanence upon the spiritual element that pervades it.

The clerk's certificate, the wedding ring, the priest's blessing, cannot make two individuals husband and wife. This ceremony is only proof to the world of the heart union already existing. It is an institution honored by law and custom for developing family life.

If love is the keynote of the union of husband and wife a harmonious adjustment of their daily lives and conduct is possible, for love is the embodiment of intelligence, and meets every condition with boundless tact and wisdom.

Love teaches that no man owns his wife, that no woman owns her husband, that in nowise can the marriage bond be construed into ownership. Love makes obedience lighter than liberty. Individual habits, individual tastes, and individual desires are recognized, and respected. *I will* and *you must* are not in love's vocabulary. The one act symbolizing union and affection, giving expression to creative life, by love's enactment, is born of desires that are mutual and participated in with equal pleasure.

The truly married consummate this union with perfect freedom and naturalness, and at the same time their hearts leap with joy as they awake to the deeper meanings of life.

The blending of the two in sexual consummation is fulfillment of law, as much as is the union of the fructifying principle in plants. Sexual instinct is not something to be killed, to be ignored, to be stamped out of existence. Man is not to become an ascetic, but rather he is to consider this sign a confirmation of his deeper relation to the entire universe, and to know that a right appropriation of the sex force is required.

Creative energy is neither for one moment to be stultified nor considered ignoble.

In Karezza they give willing obedience to love's commands, and in this union the entire nature of husband and wife blend in a communion that is fraught with calmness, self-control, justice and altruism. Each abides in the love of the other; each gives and each receives.

Reciprocity is the basis for the ethics of marriage. To give and to receive are equally virtuous. Upon this foundation principle the success of Karezza depends - one calls and the other responds; by a mutual understanding and a mutual participation, the selfish element is ruled out, and every consummation of passion becomes a true marriage sacrament which reflects upon character all that is permanent and valuable.

It gives to marriage a significance that is exalted as much above the ordinary union as human life is higher than animal life.

In abstinence save for procreation, one propagates only, while Karezza conduces to the building of character and spiritual growth, and at the same time the sexual functions are honored, refined and dignified. In this marriage there is no bondage for either man or woman; it is a result of the recognition of the spiritual nature of man, and in this recognition he is enabled so to order his life that he is master of conditions. He causes the world of matter to serve him. He not only claims and appropriates the forces of nature, but in his new strength and power, in his knowledge of the all-potent spiritual forces, he breaks the bonds of supposed fleshly limitations. In the wisdom of spiritual knowledge, he acquires the conscious ability to divert his entire nature, his thoughts, aspirations and desires into channels of effectiveness.

Desire should not be crushed and obliterated as taught by the Oriental adepts and all ascetics, but rather wisely directed and appropriated.

Desire is the prophecy of attainment. There can be no growth without it. Desire is the germ that bursts the chrysalis of inheritance and tradition; it gives wings to the spirit aiding it to overcome bodily disabilities, and to break the clanking chains of erroneous thinking. Guided and guarded by intellect and intuition, it leads to knowledge of higher truths.

Desire to drink from the source of life, love and intelligence enables one to have a glimpse of, and to experience an at-one-ment with universal principle itself.

Seek and ye shall find. Through desire marriage may be glorified, and those joined together in the highest law cannot be put asunder by any misstatements or misjudgments of men and women, nor by their own trivial errors committed in ignorance.

Each comes to know the soul of the other in its perfectness, and knows to love and honor. The love and loyalty pledged on the wedding day are nothing as compared to the love and loyalty of an open vision.

The abiding happiness fulfills the promise of the past.

In peace and reverence marriage becomes a holy bond of matrimony, a more enduring bond than can be conferred by prince, potentate or state can make or sanction. Each bears to the other a noble allegiance, not as a fetter but as a garland.

If I could present a composite photograph of the correspondence from my files, the burden of which is the secret tyranny of unrestrained passion over the lives of men and women, it would be a marvelously strong appeal to science to come to the relief of the ignorant. Not infrequently several children are born within fifteen or eighteen months of each other, from one mother, while motherhood, in its manifold functions, presents no plea to command restraint and respect from the husband. For the relief of such mothers, and to prevent similar experiences, I dip my pen in the fire of love to write. While pleading for the freedom of women and justice to children, I do not forget that man commits the wrong in ignorance.

Although his heart is full of love and a desire to bless the woman of his choice, he has never been instructed in the way. Simply and blindly has he followed the example and guidance of men equally ignorant, and accepted the traditions of *man's necessities* and woman's compulsory obedience.

Most men are true to their social, religious and political opinions, and once seeing and understanding a better way of life, they will give loyal allegiance to nobler ethics of marriage.

A mother in the far West writes:

I was a school teacher in Illinois, and was married at 22, ten years ago. I came with my husband to make a home in a new country. We endured many privations, but none so great as the separation from friends and con- genial society. The burden of child-bearing, so far from dear mother and relatives, the days and nights of agonizing fear, of anxious watching over little ones, of physical suffering, and, most of all, heart anguish, cannot be told. Dare I, can I write of my husband, he whom I adored, he who has shared his all with me? Does a man love a woman when he is not just to her? Must I stifle the cry in my heart for some response to my deeper nature?

Would death be any relief? But I put back all thoughts of death when I feel the searching trust of six pairs of eyes - and Harry! One thing, dear friend, I have never contemplated leaving him; but, alas, my own bitter experience shows me what is revealed in the divorce courts, and tell me, tell me truly, is this wrong and injustice sanctioned by God and nature? Can a man be virtuous who makes nightly demands on a woman that loathes and repulses his embrace; when either sickness or pregnancy is scarcely considered a barrier? Must I continue bearing children that we cannot clothe and educate properly, and most of all that are not born of love and desire; whose first cry seems like a wail of protest against a chance existence?

Do I weary you? I beg and plead that you may not spurn my letter unless you can give no hope, for in all the wide world there is no other to whom I dare go.

Hopefully and sincerely,

DORA S.

DEAR DORA S.:

Every graveyard is filled with monuments of experiences like yours. Dear heart, I believe there is help and salvation for you. You have given me a glimpse of your deep, abiding love for your husband, and it is through this and your ability to give him your confidence that you will find help. If he will listen to you at all, you may yet enjoy a true mar- riage on earth.

I send you the *Better Way,* by Newton. I also wish to know if you have ever heard that intercourse may be had without culmination – no emission being allowed? This naturally gives perfect control of the fecundating power. Many people practice this method, and claim the highest possible enjoyment and no loss of vitality. Your intelligence and desire will lead you to accord your lives to this latter method that has been both light and help to many others. You will, I am sure, be freed from this bondage to passion. It is a matter of control to which every person can train himself, and a road in which the intelligent are easily led. If I can serve you further, please command me.

Sincerely,

A.B.S

Nearly a year afterwards I received the following letter:

DEAR DR. S.:

I did not intend so long a time to elapse before letting you know of my deep heart-felt gratitude for your timely advice. I could repay you in no better way than to cite my experience for the benefit of others who suffer as I did, and who from unselfish motives desire and seek relief.

When I received your letter I read it at once to Harry. With a tone of impatience he said: "That is a woman's idea."

That night and days following we were both thoughtfully silent. When I had read the *Better Way*, I asked him to peruse it, saying to him: "Here is a man's idea of marriage. He seems to be a man of intelligence, and one whose opinion should command respect from those desiring to live aright. He, though a man, puts greater restrictions on conduct than the woman idea does."

"For you, Dora, I will read it, but you must not be too sure that I will accept any newfangled notions," he replied.

The book certainly interested him, for he did not retire until it was finished. The babe had been restless, and though he knew I had not slept, he never spoke a word. Days and nights passed and the subject was not broached. I felt that I had done my part, and it was for him to speak.

It came over me with an inexpressible horror that, in according our lives to Newton's theory, he felt, I was exercising a tyranny and coercion even greater than I had suffered. It had never occurred to me that Harry might think I was assuming a dictatorial attitude in the matter, for I preferred his fullest and most cordial cooperation in that relation from which he would gain equally with me. Still, I could not tell; he was attentive, often planning surprises for my comfort and happiness, unusually patient and kind with the children, but in the long days and nights never a word of love and trust.

I recalled having once heard that absence is the best test of affection." So I planned an inexpensive trip, and with my two youngest children visited a cousin twenty-five miles away.

We, Harry and I, had never been separated for even one night in almost eleven years. We soon discovered that ours was a real soul union, and that we had committed the greatest desecration by sacrificing this union to such frequent physical embraces.

Absence and the silent messenger of love, the written page, enabled us to open our hearts to each other. The long letters that followed were a renewal of courtship days, only our love seemed more sacred and hallowed by consecration to better purposes.

I must not take your time to tell you all, but you will be glad to know that we have adopted the *woman's idea,* and found it far from difficult. It seems almost strange to ourselves, but weeks often elapse without any sign of the physical demand, and we are far happier in this new life than in the old.

Harry joins me in gratitude to you.

Very sincerely,

DORA. S.

Thus many, many testify that the physical union under a wise, intellectual control leads to a true spiritual marriage, out of which develops the looked-for and expected happiness in this relation.

In obedience to the law of Karezza satiety is never known, and the married are never less than lovers; each day reveals new delights, each hour is an hour of growth, the entire life blossoms in joy and revels in golden fruitage. The common daily sarcasms of married people are at an end, the unseemly quarrels have no beginnings and the divorce courts are cheated of their records. Welcome children are born of the spirit and develop in a beneficent atmosphere of trust and harmony. The ideal family living in mutual love and helpfulness magnify the law and stand as an emblem of purity and truth.

CHAPTER IX
PROCREATION OF THOUGHT

As far as we yet know, spirit or mind is the substance,
it shows through the body – is served by the body. - Koradine.

In Karezza the procreation of thought is possible. Spirit is the *ego,* the higher self, the Divine principle in man that expresses his unity with all nature. The reader will remember that we said that soul is spirit in action.

Soul is the "spiritual body" mentioned by Saint Paul; it bears a more intimate relation to the physical body than a hand does to a glove.

It is in the soul that all the activities of our being are exerted, the movement of muscles, the processes of digestion and nutrition all occur as manifestations of the spiritual or soul nature. It is in the soul that we find the senses, here all feeling is experienced, all knowledge acquired; character is fashioned and power of choice occurs.

In the soul all the activities of our being are impelled. The movement of muscles, the processes of digestion and nutrition all occur as manifestations of the spiritual or soul nature. It is in the soul that we find the senses and emotions. The soul also has the power of choice, and the ability to fashion character. Every soul has a dual nature, the masculine and feminine; intellect and wisdom characterizing the male, intuition and affection the female. These are existent to some degree in every human being. Grindon says: "All that belongs to thought, understanding or mind, is masculine; all that belongs to will, intuition, affection of heart, is feminine."

When one acts immediately from the intellectual principle, manliness is foremost, when from the will principle, womanliness. The most consistent, perfect personality is one in which both the male and the female principles are harmoniously developed. Since sex is of the soul, is it not possible that as spiritual unity develops, thought may be procreated? That would mean a procreation on the spiritual plane of ideas and theories to be practically developed for the good of the world.

The physical relation may or may not be of value for this higher procreation. It has been proven that in the Karezza relation the creative principle becomes active in both husband and wife. While the spiritual senses are thus attuned to the finest perception in soul vibration, ideas of great moment are conceived. It is within the power of men and women, interested in the operation of spiritual law, further to demonstrate the validity of the theory.

Newton says: "It is important to know that there are other uses for the procreative element than the generation of physical offspring, far better uses than its waste in momentary pleasure. It may, indeed, be better wasted than employed in imposing unwelcome burdens on toilworn and outraged women. But there should be no waste. This element when retained in the system may be coined into new thoughts, perhaps new inventions, grand conceptions of the true, the beautiful, the useful; or into fresh emotions of joy, and impulses of kindness and blessing to all around. This is, in fact, but another department of procreation. It is the procreation of thoughts, ideas, feelings of good will, intuitions of truth - that is, it is procreation on the mental and spiritual planes, instead of physical. It is just as really a part of the generative function as is the begetting of physical offspring. It is by far the greater part, for physical procreation can ordinarily be participated in but seldom; while mental and spiritual procreation may and should go on perpetually through all our earthly lives - yea, through all our immortal existence."

To the mature man a consecration of virile powers is essential to the maintenance of a high tone of vitality and of manly vigor. On it depends the degree of positive or impregnative force which characterizes the individual in his mental activities.

A speaker or writer who is addicted to waste in this department, though he may talk and write with great profuseness, may expect that his words will be comparatively powerless in their effect upon others. They will lack germinating power. But he who conserves this element, in a calm, deliberate union, charges not only his words, but the very atmosphere, with a power which penetrates and begets new thoughts and new emotions in those whom he addresses.

"Every idea is an intellectual child, and if it be a pleasant thing to have physical sons and daughters, what are the power, the opulence, the enjoyments of him who abounds in ideas, the beautiful and immortal sons and daughters of the soul?"

Who, then, are the true old bachelors and old maids, and who the really childless? Not so much the unmarried by ring and book, as they who have not courted and wedded nature, receiving from her in reply a family of beautiful ideas.

He is a spiritual parent who has learned to drink from the well of truth, and from the deep resources of his being, has discovered the secret powers of life. In outward manifestation he may preach, teach, heal and prophesy, but should he sit quietly in his own home, his life is a silent benediction to all, even to those who do not come into his presence. His creative energy brings forth according to the potent power of thinking.

Through the contagion of thought his influence has infinite possibilities.

Spiritual pleasures transcend those of a physical nature, and all practices that lead one to walk in the paths of light and truth con- duce to peace and harmony. Not only this, but through the laws that govern the occult forces - in the practice of Karezza, there are far more reaching results than accrue to the individual in the ordinary sexual relation.

Long ago Laboulaye asserted that" the passions take the place in the soul which the will does not occupy, and there may yet be discovered a process by which passion may be transmuted into intellectual fibre. This is, indeed, the last and highest possibility of human culture."

People will know this place, the functions of passion, and their relations to the will when they understand the germinating power of thought and have their sexual life under a wise control. Men and women practicing Karezza attest that their very souls in union take on a procreating power, and that it seems to have an impregnating force, far transcending in power and intelligence any ordinary thought force. These mighty soul conceptions demand generation and birth, for the world is in need of their regenerating power. Let all children of men listen for these messages. Let them go into the hush of the spirit and wait in the night stillness for the revelation. It may come in the fire of a poet or the eloquence of an orator, but certainly if souls are attuned to life's harmonies the law will be fulfilled in song and prophecy.

This silence is not mere silence of sound, but even thought is hushed, the eyes forget to see and the ears forget to hear, only spirit listens to spirit. It is as Koradine describes when Tommy was healed: "Then came a deep, deep stillness that cleansed and hushed all thought, for there was no need of thought, no room for speech; just stillness, stillness."

In this ecstatic stillness the problems of the philanthropist are solved; the sculptor's marble glows with life; the painter's canvas reflects love and intelligence; while the desires of each are lifted to the highest and truest expressions of the soul, expressions that shall hasten the universal brotherhood of man.

CHAPTER X

SPIRITUAL GROWTH

I well perceive how in thine intellect already shines the eternal light, which once seen, always kindles love. - Dante.

Souls really united progress unitedly. This is the strongest and greatest argument of this altruistic union. The highest aim in life should be spiritual development and attainment of power and strength in this direction. Habits and conditions that contribute to this should be sought. Miller says:

With Zugassent's Discovery (Karezza) comes also the one, supreme truth, that its greatest crown of honor consists in its conducing to the highest and noblest spiritual development.

What is spiritual development? It is coming into recognition of the supremacy of the spiritual over the physical; it is conscious mastery in one sense, and in another it is a knowledge of the God-like in man that takes possession of him, leading and guiding him in all the walks of life.

It is true that in Karezza one experiences growth in the spiritual nature. This is obtained through the habit of self-control and mastery, and through the desire of each for the best good of the other, and to the high aspirations accompanying the relation.

Once having experience in Karezza, one will never return to the ordinary habits in which sensuality and selfishness so often predominate.

All spiritual experience is growth in the knowledge of man's divinity, of his inseparable union with the omnipresent principle of life. He may come to a sudden awakening of this great truth of his being which results in an instantaneous conversion, like Saul of Tarsus, or it may more slowly dawn upon his perception as in the case of Saul of old as he listened to the divine harmonies of David's harp.

Whenever and however man perceives this truth, it is borne upon his inner consciousness that the real enduring things of life belong to the spirit, while the evanescent, fleeting, unstable things of life are of the material. He comes to rule his life according to this knowledge, and while he lives in the world, he is not of it, and all things present new meanings to him.

In no part of life's domain are these new meanings more clearly perceived than in the reproductive powers. In the loving companionship of husband and wife, in the conception and birth of spiritual and physical offspring - in all their innermost relations, their lives are attuned to nature's harmonies, their very existence vibrates with the divine unity of the universe.

Both men and women can train this cre- ative energy into power. *The word is the sword of the spirit.* It is a well proven law that the reiteration of a thought brings about a condition which makes manifest what the thought expresses. Therefore, let one repeat again and again, "I am a creator, not merely of human children, but creator of thoughts, of ideas and of resources. I devote my great heart-love to the interests of the world. There is no task too onerous for my devotion, no service too difficult for my undertaking. All children are mine, all interests are mine, gladly and cheerfully I answer the call to serve those who need me. I am both father and mother. In joy and gladness do I consecrate myself to the world."

In this prayer of faith and fulfillment one recognizes the power of the omnipotent creative life principle, and in beneficence and freedom experiences a vivifying stimulant to works of love.

Here is given a glimpse of the greatest spiritual law yet discovered. It is a key to self-training for power and mastery. It is power itself. This theory is not based upon denials, and the asceticisms of all religious teachings of the past. Oriental philosophers and western theologians have usually united in counseling people to kill out desire and passion. The Nirvana of existence and the sanctification of saints is alike to be beyond ambition and desire. On the contrary, the philosophy of today expounds a law of affirmation in which one attains development of the *self* in power, together with a systematic consecration of all aspirations and faculties.

We are living spiritual beings. Claiming this, we enter consciously into our possessions, understanding that we have creative powers born of the spirit. By wise appropriation of them we become superior to bodily conditions, until they wheel into line and serve us. We become greater than anything with which we have to deal. We enthrone the *ego,* which is spirit, and utilize something of the divine potency which has been hidden by human limitations and erroneous thinking. Man has been bound by ignorance, but he comes through development and spiritual consciousness to know his power.

As God, life and law become synonymous in the student's mind, physical and spiritual science join hands in demonstrating the problems of existence.

No wider field of exploration is presented to the discoverer of nature's secrets than that of marital ethics. Groveling in the darkness of ignorance and superstition, man has hitherto closed to himself the doors of investigation, labeling them unclean.

Henceforth purity guards the entrance, and wisdom demands that youth shall not be deprived of the benefits of the experience of those who have knowledge to give. Instead of associating creative life and energy with things base and unclean, man will set all his thoughts to words as bright and enduring as the stars, and they will be the light, love and intelligence that guide his feet.

If we can perceive beauty in everything of God's doings we may argue that we have reached the true perception of universal law. – Ruskin

CORROBORATION[3]

TESTIMONY OF A YOUNG LADY MISSIONARY

The following correspondence was originally published in Creative Life - a brochure now out of print. It is reproduced here as especially corroborative of theories advanced in Chapters I and X, and no doubt will be

---

[3] [From the earlier edition of *Karezza*]

Facts corroborating any new theory or habit of life are always in demand. As Karezza is comparatively new to many and as the results of its adoption will be far reaching upon the lives of men and women, it is due the reader that the theories and principles taught in this work be substantiated by testimony from intelligent people, who, unprejudiced, give their experience for the benefit of others.

If some have derived happiness and satisfaction from the course herein proposed others may. Of course it may require self training and greater knowledge of the laws of life; therefore, if questions arise, or in any way the subject does not seem clear, or if men or women desire reading that will aid their understanding, the author holds herself in readiness to give such aid. It is right understanding and right application of truth that should be sought.

ALICE B. STOCKHAM, M. D.,

Evanston, Ill. March 1896

read with interest and profit:

DEAR DR. STOCKHAM: - When I read your book, TOKOLOGY, and looked at your portrait, I felt that I had found one in whom I could confide, and from whom I might hope for real help.

Very early in life I became addicted to a bad, secret habit. It does not seem as if I ever learned it. I seemed always to have had it; nor did I know I was doing wrong until about eighteen years of age, when my conscience seemed to tell me it was not right. I was a professing Christian, and I began to feel any secret propensity, no matter what the pleasure it gave, could not be right.

Sometime after I read of the fearful results that would follow this habit; I soon decided I must stop. I made up my mind to conquer the habit solely by my own will power, but utterly failed. Humbled, I sought Divine help; but for a long time it seemed that to stop the sun in his course would prove as easy a task as to abandon the habit entirely.

At twenty-two, a year after graduating, I went out to China as a missionary. For more than two years I realized what it was to be kept by the power of God; but like many a drunkard, I began to think I was safe, and neglected to be as watchful and prayerful as I should have been, and, being overtaken by temptation, yielded several times. I know the desire is still there, and what I want to know is this:

What course of treatment will succeed in destroying the desire?

Should I entertain the idea of marriage?

What effect will the past have upon the marriage relation?

I do not expect to be married for a year or more. My intended husband is also a missionary. I am in perfect health, but have a poor memory. I take frequent baths and live an abstemious life. Please advise me at___. If you can offer any relief, I shall always be

    Gratefully yours,

          C.

To this earnest appeal I sent this reply:

DEAR MISS C. : - I thank you most sincerely for your confidence. There certainly must be help for you as you so greatly desire it. I think you

50

would not have had such a struggle if you had understood that passion is simply the evidence or sign of creative power. It does not follow that this creative power should be devoted to procreation, but it may be used in any good work.

Now, according to your attitude of mind, will be your experience. When the feeling comes on, say, 'Yes, I know I am a creator. What am I to do?' It may be to form plans, help another, to teach school, to build a home, whatever comes before you in your life work. Respond quickly. At once think out your plans, create, and lo! what you call temptation is gone. It is a call from God. Do you know we are wrong in attaching baseness to these feelings? Get that idea out of your mind.

The treatment most surely lies in following the law. Turn your creative power to good uses, to *tremendous* uses, if need be. Your consecration to good work is all right, now consecrate especially your creative powers. Every indication of passion must be treated as a call from God for some new work - some creation. Put your mind to work to know what it is.

It is not the body that calls; it is the spirit, and *obedience* is *the cure.*

Say over and over again, 'I am a creator. What am I to produce?' Listen, listen, and God will answer.

Yours sincerely,

A.

No letter ever gave me such real joy as her answer. Believing that the perusal of it will be helpful to many, I quote with the writer's permission:

DEAR DOCTOR: Your letter was received sev- eral weeks ago when I was away on a tour speaking at missionary meetings.

Really, I do not know when I have been at such a loss for words as I am in finding any that will correctly and sufficiently express my gratitude for what you have done for me.

For a long time I have thought that the work of the Christian physician is such a noble one that it is second only to that of the Christian minister and missionary. Since receiving your letter it has seemed as though I might go farther than that, and place it *before* that of the Christian ministry; but perhaps it would be more correct to feel that, in your particular case, both offices are combined, for who could better minister to the soul, or teach a spiritual truth of more vital importance than you have done in my case?

As I read and re-read that part of your letter in relation to the cure, and began to comprehend its full meaning and bearing, I felt as I have done at important crises of my life when some new spiritual truth has fully dawned upon me, and I have taken a great stride in the Christian life, and my feeling towards you was more than that of gratitude and admiration. You have done me good *for life,* as you have done many others, and who knows how much good to future generations?

Were I to send you five times the amount you charged, you would be no more nearly paid for what you have done for me than by the amount named. I take the knowledge gained as a gift from God, through you, His agent, realizing that thereby my responsibility is increased, and knowing that from Him you will receive your reward.

All being well, I shall be married at home in August and return at once to China. I may go by Chicago. If I should do so, I might say that it would be a very great gratification to me to have the honor of meeting you and the privilege of thanking you in person for what you have done for me. Sincerely yours,

C.

===========

The following is from a personal friend, eminent as a teacher of metaphysical philosophy:

I thank you, Dear Doctor, for the perusal of Karezza in manuscript. God bless you - I know it is true. I have had experience that has proved it to my satisfaction. To me the experience is very sacred, but if it aids to lift the veil (or chain) of animalism from the hearts of women and men and thus open the realm to spiritual possibilities, I have no objection to your using it. ...

I should say we had for months talked over together this problem, with its possible results. With our deep love for each other, and our love and interest for humanity we wished no theory to be left unproven.

Each of us had made a close study of the Science of Being, so we well understood the power of thought, and knew that the mind must consent before the simplest act in life can be performed. This was our theory: Man and woman are opposite to and counterpart of each other, as Tennyson beautifully expresses it:

> For woman is not undeveloped man,
> But diverse -
> Not like to like, but like in difference,
> Yet in the long years liker must they grow;
> The man be more of woman, she of man;
> He gain in sweetness and in moral height,
> She mental breadth, -
> Till at last she set herself to man,
> Like perfect music unto noble words;
> Self-reverent each and reverencing each,
> Distinct in individualities;
> But like each other ev'n as those who love.
> Then comes the statelier Eden back to man;
> Then reign the world's great bridals, chaste
> and calm;
> Then springs the crowning race of humankind.
> May these things be!

So then we said that man might fully appreciate woman, and that woman might fully appreciate man. To do this it is necessary that they adjust themselves on a spiritual plane, that he may be more a woman in nature and she more a man, and yet maintain the secret of their individuality....

To make the experiment complete, for several successive cohabitations we kept the physical under complete control - at no time allowing a crisis.

We found that neither one was disturbed in any physical sense. There was no uneasiness, no unrest, no unsatisfied desire, rather on the contrary the satisfaction was complete, resulting in a beautiful rest and a sweet sleep seldom experienced. Each occasion was indeed a sacrament.

I feel confident however that this particular relation could not have been satisfactory had we not known the power of the mind over the body. We were fortified and prepared for each occasion. We fixed our minds on and expected spiritual attainment. The result was perfectly successful. We had previously agreed upon the duration (the complete union not more than thirty minutes) and that there must not be a desire on the part of one which the other would not readily meet. Following the relation, side by side, in the beautiful stillness, I experienced a peace, a perfect satisfaction passing mortal understanding. I was lifted up and up. I seemed to go into the realm of spirit - clairvoyant, intensely so - not to behold *spirits,* but rather spiritual possibilities. Indeed it hath not entered into the heart of man to conceive all the things prepared for him, with the proper appropriation of creative energy.

To those seeking knowledge from the spirit of truth, my name may be given. To all others I am,

Sincerely,

SIGMA.,Chicago, Feb. 8, 1896.

==========

In *Male Continence,* a pamphlet now out of print, after giving a graphic and eloquent plea for the rights of the child, the writer says:

The discovery was occasioned and even forced upon me by a very sorrowful experience. In the course of six years my wife went through the agonies of five births. Four of them were premature. Only one child lived. This experience was what directed my studies and kept me studying. After our last disappointment I pledged my word to my wife that I would never again expose her to such fruitless suffering. I made up my mind to live apart from her, rather than break this promise. I conceived the idea that the sexual organs have a social function which is distinct from the propagative function, and that these functions may be separated practically. I experimented on this idea, and found that the self-control which it requires is not difficult; that my enjoyment was increased; that my wife's experience was very satisfactory, as it had never been before; that we had escaped the horrors and fear of involuntary propagation. This was a great deliverance. It made a happy household. I communicated my discovery to a friend. His experience and that of his household were the same. In normal condition, men are entirely competent to choose in sexual intercourse whether they will stop at any point in the voluntary stages of it, and so make it simply an act of communion, or go through to the involuntary stage, and make it an act of propagation.

The situation may be compared to a stream in three conditions, viz.:
1.   a fall;
2.   a course of rapids above the fall; and
3.   still water above the rapids.

The skillful boatman may choose whether he will remain in the still water, or venture more or less down the rapids, or run his boat over the fall. But there is a point on the verge of the fall where he has no control over his course; and just above that, there is a point where he will have to struggle with the current in a way which will give his nerves a severe trial, even though he may escape the fall. If he is willing to learn, experience will teach him the wisdom of confining his excursions to the region of easy rowing, unless he has an object in view that is worth the cost of going over the falls.

You have now our whole theory. It consists in analyzing sexual intercourse, recognizing in it two distinct acts, the social and the propagative, which can be separated practically, and affirming that it is best, not only with reference to prudential considerations, but for immediate pleasure, that a man should content himself with the social act, except when he intends procreation.

(1) It does not seek to prevent the intercourse of sexes, but rather to prevent that which generally puts an end to such intercourse. (2) It does not seek to prevent the natural effects of the propagative act, but to prevent the propagative act itself except when it is intended to be effectual. (3) Of course it does not seek to destroy the living results of the propagative act, but provides that impregnation and child-bearing shall be voluntary, and therefore desired.

And now to speak affirmatively, the exact thing that our theory does propose is, to take that same power of moral restraint and self-control which Paul, Malthus, the Shakers, and all considerate men use in one way or another to limit propagation, and instead of applying it, as they do, to the prevention of the intercourse of the sexes, to introduce it at another stage of proceedings, viz., after the sexes have come together in social effusion, and before they have reached the propagative crisis; thus allowing the most essential freedom of love, and at the same time avoiding undesired procreation and all the other evils incident to male incontinence.

The objection urged to this method is, that it is unnatural, and unauthorized by the example of other animals. I may answer that cooking, wearing clothes, living in houses, and almost everything else done by civilized man, is unnatural in the same sense, and that a close adherence to the example of the brutes would require us to forego speech and go on all fours! But, on the other hand, if it is natural in the best sense, as I believe it is, for rational beings to forsake the example of the brutes and improve nature by invention and discovery in all directions, then truly the argument turns the other way, and we shall have to confess that until men and women find a way to elevate their sexual functions above those of the brutes, by introducing into them self-control and moral culture, they are living in unnatural degradation.

But I will come closer to this objection. The real meaning of it is that it is a difficult interruption of a natural act. But every instance of self-denial is an interruption of some natural act. The man who virtuously contents himself with a look at a beautiful woman is conscious of such an interruption. The lover who stops at a kiss denies himself a natural progression. It is an easy descending grade through all the approaches of sexual love from the first touch of respectful friendship to the final complete amalgamation. Must there be no interruption of this natural slide? Brutes, animal or human, tolerate none. Shall their ideas of self-denial prevail? Nay, it is the glory of man to control himself, and the Kingdom of Heaven summons him to self-control in ALL THINGS. If it is noble and beautiful for a betrothed lover to respect the law of marriage in the midst of the glories of courtship, it may be even more noble and beautiful for the wedded lover to respect the laws of health and propagation in the midst of the ecstasies of sexual union. The same moral culture that ennobles the antecedents and approaches of marriage will some time surely glorify the consummation.

The method of controlling propagation which results from our argument is natural, healthy and effectual.

The useless expenditure of seed certainly is not natural. God cannot have designed that men should sow seed by the wayside where they do not expect it to grow, nor in the same field where it has already been sown and is growing; and yet such is the practice of men in the ordinary sexual relation. They sow seed habitually where they do not wish it to grow. This is wasteful of life and cannot be natural. Yet is it not manifest that the instinct of our nature demands congress of the sexes, not only for propagative, but for social and spiritual purposes? The act of propagation should be reserved for its legitimate occa- sions when conception is intended. The idea that sexual intercourse, limited to the social part of it, is impossible or difficult, and therefore not natural, is contradicted by the experience of many. Abstinence from masturbation is impossible or difficult where habit has made it a second nature, and yet no one will say that habitual masturbation is natural. So abstinence from the propagative part of sexual intercourse may seem impracticable to depraved natures, and yet be perfectly natural and easy to persons properly trained to chastity. Our method simply proposes the subordination of *the flesh to the spirit,* teaching men to seek principally the elevated spiritual pleasures of sexual connection. This is certainly natural and easy to the spiritual man however difficult it may be to the sensual.

In the first place it secures woman from the curses of involuntary and undesirable procreation; and secondly, it stops the drain of life on the part of the man.

The habit of making sexual intercourse a quiet affair, restricting the action of the organs to such limits as are necessary to the avoidance of the crisis, can easily be established, and then there is no risk of conception without intention.

Our theory, separating the amative from the propagative, not only relieves us of involuntary and undesirable procreation, but opens the way to scientific propagation. We believe that propagation, rightly conducted and kept within such limits as life can fairly afford, is a blessing. A very large proportion of all children born under the present system are begotten contrary to the wishes of both parents, and lie nine months in the mother's womb under their mother's curse or a feeling little better than a curse. Such children cannot be well organized. We are opposed to excessive, and consequently, oppressive procreation, which is almost universal. We are opposed to random procreation, which is unavoidable in the present marriage custom. But we favor intelligent, well- ordered procreation.

We believe the time will come when involuntary and random propagation will cease, and when scientific combination will be applied to human generation as freely and successfully as it is to that of other animals. And at all events, we believe that good sense and benevolence will very soon sanction and enforce the rule that women shall bear children only when they choose. They have the principal burden of breeding to bear, and they, rather than men, should have their choice of time and circumstances.

===========

Strike of the Sex, by Geo. N. Miller, has been read by thousands.[4] He writes:

To the teachers of the young, Zugassent's Discovery appeals with the voice of a prophet. It concerns the happiness of millions yet to be. If it were taught to the young by enlightened and pure- minded teachers they would never be conscious of any sacrifice. On the contrary, they would prefer it, as has been demonstrated; and the tremendous compensations which such a wise conservation of force would bring would speedily make the earth astir with a new prepotent race.

Those who perceive the crying need for a radical reformation in existing beliefs on sexual subjects, must look to the instruction of the *young* for the step in advance they earnestly hope to see.

Let the young be taught that it was never nature's intention that man should take pride in his purely animal instincts and desires, and that the progress of the race depends more upon the absolute control of the sexual nature for the improvement of the species than upon any other one thing except the broadest idea of human brotherhood.

Let them be taught that the organs for love's expression are entirely distinct from those of generation, and that it is an unworthy act to use the latter except for nature's purposes; that the *proper* use of the former raises the sexual act to a mental plane where it ceases to be the brutalizing and degrading animalism it often is, but becomes the next step toward soul development which is the appointed task of man.

And indeed, if a discerning public sentiment could be formed, and the young could be taught by pure-minded teachers, that it would be far better for their own health and happiness, as well as that of their posterity, to regulate their lives by this rule of temperance, a great many happy marriages would be possible which are now cruelly postponed or hopelessly abandoned for fear of the expense and embarrassment of children. It considers the welfare and happiness of others in the most engrossing of human pleasures, and thus partakes of the

---

[4] Zugassent's Discovery is the same theory of control as Karezza.

divine. It lifts the interchanges between the sexes from the purely sensual plane, tending toward death, into that of joyous social and religious fellowship tending toward life. It envelops those who really apprehend it in an atmosphere of purity and chastity sweeter and far more real than that possessed by nuns.

There is today among pure-minded people who believe that the sexual nature is sacred, holy, and glorious, a crying and insistent demand for a pure and innocent method of limiting the size of their families and mitigating the woes of poverty and ill- health resulting from too frequent child-- bearing. Conscientious and God-fearing persons naturally recoil from the methods adopted by the irreligious. They cannot feel that such methods have the justifying and ennobling effect which should pertain to the associations of a sacrament. And shall such people as these be always left to misdirection, chance, and misery? Do not the infinite resources of Christianity contain an assured cure for this evil? Here is one that seems completely to supply this demand. It is not only intrinsically pure and innocent, but in teaching self-control and true temperance, without asceticism, it reacts powerfully for good on the whole character. It is not a merely nugatory device, but a stimulus to spirituality.

The young people who are now approaching marriageable age live in a world whose ideas, in nearly every department of life, have been largely modified, if not completely changed, by the advent of steam, electricity, the microscope, the telescope, the telephone, and other constantly multiplying agents of enlightenment. Is it not reasonable to suppose that there is the same opportunity for infinite improvement and revolu- tionizing discovery in such a vital department as that of the sex relation, and that the results of such discovery will be commensurate with the immense importance of the subject? The Discovery of Zugassent has been demonstrated to be such an improvement, and it alone provides a sure foundation for the perfect solution both of the sexual and population problems.

The final supremacy over nature lies in the full subjection of man's own body to his intelligent will. There are already an abundance of familiar facts showing the influence of education and direct discipline in developing the powers of the body. We see men every day who, by attention and painstaking investigation and practice in some mechanical art, have gained a power over their muscles, for certain purposes, which to the mere natural man would be impossible or miraculous. In music the great violinists and pianists are examples. All the voluntary faculties are known to come under the power of education, and the human will is found able to express itself in the motions of the body, to an extent and perfection that is in proportion to the painstaking and discipline that are applied. So far as the department of voluntary outward habits is concerned, the influence of will and education to control the body is universally admitted. But there is a step further. Investigation and experience are now ready to demonstrate the power of the will over what have been considered and called the *involuntary* processes of the body. The mind can take control of them, certainly, to a great extent; the later discoveries point to the conclusion, that there are strictly no *involuntary* departments in the human system, but that every part falls appropriately and in fact within the dominion of mind, spirit, and will.[5]

As a promoter of domestic happiness and a preventer of the woes that lead to divorce, Zugassent's Discovery is entitled to the lasting gratitude of all good people, as is shown by the many testimonies on record, two of which follow:

Since my husband became acquainted with the philosophy of Zugassent, he has endeared himself to me a hundredfold, and although our so called 'honeymoon' was passed five years ago, it was no more real, and far less lasting,

than the ecstatic, the unspeakable happiness which is now continually mine. My prosaic and sometimes indifferent husband has changed by a heavenly magic into an ardent and entrancing lover, for

---

[5] Those familiar with the writings of Henry Wood, W. F. Evans, Ursula N. Gestefeld and a host of others will see that G. N. Miller hints only at fundamental truths that are in everyday usage and guidance for thousands of people.

whose coming I watch with all the tender raptures of a schoolgirl. His very step sends a thrill through me, for I know that my beloved will grasp me and clasp me and cover me with kisses such as only the most enthusiastic lover could give. And though the years lapse, I cannot see or feel any change in the way he cherishes me. To each other we are continual objects of deepest reverence and the most sacred mystery. Our affection deepens, our romance seems as sure and enduring as the stars. My lover! my hero! my knight! my husband! I date my marriage from the time when he became a disciple of Zugassent, for that was the beginning of our assured happiness.

But it is not alone as a cherishing lover that my husband has become my crown of happiness. He has grown perceptibly nobler in character, in purpose; in strength, in all the qualities that make a man God-like, so that beside a lover I have a strong friend and wise counselor, and my happiness is complete. L.S.

I am a young man, 24 years of age, enjoying the most vigorous health. For two years after becoming engaged I delayed marriage, simply because I did not think my income sufficient to support a wife and the children which I regarded as an inevitable consequence. Happily for me a friend, who knew my circumstances, wrote me about Zugassent's Discovery. The ideas contained in this discovery were so different from all my preconceived ideas of what constituted marital happiness, that I was inclined to reject them as utterly impracticable and absurd. But the more I thought of the matter the more clearly I saw that if there was a possibility of these new ideas being true, they were exactly adapted to a man in my circumstances, and that they made my marriage immediately practicable. The wholly new thought that retaining the vital force within himself would naturally make a man stronger, cleaner, and better also seemed to me not irrational. With some misgivings, therefore, I determined to venture upon marriage, and it has been completely successful. I have had a continuous honeymoon for four years. I have never been conscious of any irksome restraint or asceticism in my sexual experience; and my self-control and strength, mental and physical, have greatly increased since my marriage. In the light of my own experience I regard the idea that the seminal fluid is a secretion that must be got rid of as being the most pernicious and fatal one that can possibly be taught to young people.

J. G.

===========

My Dear Dr. Stockham:

Your most gracious answer to my request came promptly. Last evening I devoted to Karezza and Creative Life. I bless you from my heart for this beautiful interpretation of the relation between the sexes. Passion has always seemed to me to be a sharing of God's creative life and a divine instinct. Its perversion and sensuality have profaned the holiest joys, and veiled souls from one another, shutting out the Love, which is the very High Priest of the Holy of Holies. All Womankind should give living praise and thanks for the beneficence of Karezza's influence, as I do.

It is delightful and reassuring to find one's own truest intuitions purely interpreted on an open page. My own nature is filled and vibrant with that creative fire. I have never been ashamed of it, but it has been strongly repressed. I give to my ministry the love-forces that have never been satisfied except by the transfusion of the Universal Love. I believe that the ennoblement of this passion to its own spiritual plane will lift the whole race heavenward and redeem the home and social world from retrogression. It is the divine regeneration, the new birth of Spiritual Consciousness, for which the world has suffered long and long. Permit me to express my admiration for the dignity, purity and sweet seriousness of style of Karezza and the booklets.

Accept my very real thanks.

Believe that I shall try to promote, in all ways that a sister minister may, your beneficent message to women.

Yours sincerely, for love and purity,

M.L.L.

Fort Collins, Colorado, November, 1900

Dear Dr. Stockham:

My dear wife and I are indeed very grateful for the valuable advice so freely given in your letter and in the books, which accompanied it. You will be glad to know that the information enabled us to consummateour marriage in a very beautiful way - and we are stilllovers, with extended opportunities for showing our affection and devotion for each other. I can truthfully add that the beautiful simile used in your letter of two lives flowing together like waters is applicable to us, and as we think, will be so to theend.

Acting on your advice before marriage, we read together Karezza and two of the other books you sent. My dear one was much interested and imbued by your uplifting teaching and the new ideals, which it opened up for her. Your excellent WEDDING NIGHT and the most advanced of the other books I thought best that she should read by herself, and she now desires me to express to you her heartiest thanks for the former especially, as it gives her just the information she wanted and which she had not been able to obtain elsewhere. She wishes that the WEDDING NIGHT could be placed in the hands of every prospective bride, as she is quite sure it would save much suffering and misunderstanding at the very beginning of married life.

Yours sincerely,

J.A.L.

Birmingham, England, March 28, 1901

Dear Dr. Stockham:

I want to say that I knew of, believed in, and practiced Karezza long before I knew there was such a book, and still believe it most fully.

The teachings of Karezza came to me in a critical and trying time of my life. I had been married several years, and the harmony between my wife and self seemed dying out. She had loved me dearly, but the

64

old sex embrace had no attraction for her, and grew more and more repulsive. The new teaching brought us into a new heaven and a new earth.

I cannot tell you how happy we became. We were simply lovers, but such lovers as we had never been before. An indescribable tenderness pervaded all our relations. My wife proved a sexual power and perfection rare and wonderful. Her mental and moral nature both developed until I hardly knew her, and I for the first time was sure that I was a poet. And all this ever increased until her death some years after.

Karezza seems to me to be the sex blending of the moral natures, it seems to call out and arouse to an ecstasy of delight and power the spiritual and poetic nature of both man and woman. It gives strength as if it were the key to unlock powers.

Karezza is perfectly successful where the two come together with a mutual loving desire to assist and bless each other, to blend and exchange spiritual gifts, to inspire each other to the noblest moods. Then the "Heaven" stage is easily reached.

J.W.L.
March, 1901

My Dear Dr. Stockham:

A sweet and wise American friend has introduced my dear husband and myself to the pure delights of Karezza, and I should feel myself the basest of ingrates if I left this land without writing you this word of *heartfelt thanks*; and yet how *poor* words are to convey real gratitude! We rob words of meaning by our wretched way of using them to express paltry things, and when a benefit has been done one, which enriches - nay, transforms life - the whole world - one has but the same old exhausted words.

For this wonderful discovery is in sober reality a transformer of wedded life. I am a woman of passion (until now I have always been ashamed of it). My dear husband is a man of passion; until now it has seemed that it was the one blemish on his noble manhood.
How ignorant - nay, how wicked - it all seems now.

But, my dear Dr. Stockham, how does it happen that the most mighty, the most beautiful of the natural desires - that which is at the very foundation of society, and which is connected with all the sanctities of life - marriage, with all it *ideally* means, motherhood - fatherhood - why is it that this powerful and holy passion has remained under a kind of ban?

Why, we have taken up the latent capacity which is in us for music and have trained and refined it till it ministers now to every highest thing in us, and also affords us the purest pleasure. What a distance from the savage's tom-tom to a modern piano - from the discordant savage chant to the intermezzo! We no longer eat with our fingers, tearing half-roasted flesh as we squat about a fire, but have taken up the natural desire for food and made it minister to the sweetest social pleasures. We have put thought and skill and fancy and art to work to lift eating into a great rational pleasure and refinement. And now Karezza has come! How numberless are the benefits! The first and greatest is that, at last, after nine years of *legal* marriage (and of real love, too), we are really married. There is not a *film* of constraint, false modesty, or conventionality between us, and with the downfall of the *physical* barrier has come such a flowing together of *soul* as I cannot describe. I really have never known my darling until now. He seems to me more beautiful than ever did the Apollo, and so grand and manly in his continence and self-control, while it is perfectly evident that just I - his nine years' wife, and twice a mother - am a delight to him, and oh, how *satisfying* are now the days of happy anticipation and then the happier fulfillment. Oh, dear joy-giving Dr. Stockham, what satisfaction must be yours as you think how (to thousands, I suppose), you have brought the purest, truest joys of marriage - the real nobility of self-control! Yes, you have brought to light *true marriage*, and true womanhood as well. I am no longer conscious of being a separate being, ministering to the "animal" desires of my husband as he ministered to mine. We are taught to dance, to play upon the harpsichord, to embroider, to govern servants, to enter and leave a room properly, but never how to be *wives*. It is as if we should teach officers how to bow and to dance, but not how to fight. The things worthy of the highest possible development are "left to Nature." Why do we not leave manners and eating and art to Nature?

Those who have an idea of suppressing passion are fatally wrong - vain endeavor - instead of using and giving it its regnant place. Sir J. and I have had no surer revelation in or hours of spiritual exaltation, through controlled union, than that this passion which God as made strongest and upon which is builded the family and social order, is also a *nexus* of spirit, soul and body. Every power, every emotion, every resource of the volitional life, blend with every thrilling nerve of the physical life in the controlled union.

One of the blissful results of this *vita nuova*, is that we both are perfectly unmoved by others. We are sovereigns in the sphere of our own personal beings. No other crosses the frontier.

Very warmly yours,
(Lady) J.G.C.

===========

Every person has a right to health, and most especially to that health which gives normal expression of the reproductive functions. Karezza is not an idle theory, as the above testimonials and the experience of many thousands prove. It is rather a philosophy which is attainable, and which in practice gives most satisfactory results.

It is a conscious use of the law of life in regeneration, which not only gives a knowledge of innate powers, and becomes a factor in personal development, but gives a prophecy of progeny that must surpass the most brilliant of all time.

A.B. Stockham, MD

Epilogue

Alice Bunker Stockham (1833-1912) was an obstetrician and gynecologist from Chicago, an enthusiastic fighter for a marital and sexual reform. She took *"Karezza"* from the Italian term *"carezza"* (written with a "c") meaning petting or gentle stroking. Stockham was the fifth woman in the U.S.A., who got the degree of a Medical Doctor. Apart from her special field gynecology and obstetrics she was engaged in charity and interested in spiritual topics. She also practiced homeopathy, fought against alcoholism, served probably sometimes as a trance medium and was an active feminist, a suffragette. In 1886, she published a book on the health of women: "Tokology. A Book for Every Woman" with several editions and translations into foreign languages. Leo Tolstoy, a supporter of her ideas and a personal friend of her, was so impressed, that he initiated a translation of the book into Russian and wrote a preface. He supported her approach wholeheartedly. In 1900, she published by her own press the study "Tolstoi—A Man of Peace", together with the Tolstoy study of Havelock Ellis, the well-known English sexologist.

Stockham adhered to the so called "New Thought Movement". In 1886, she joined the first course on Christian Science organised by Emma Hopkins in Chicago. Many renowned women supported this movement, which was separated into two parties. One party refused strictly any sex appeal, whereas the other one backed by Stockham tried to let it worthily perform. In 1896, she published in her own press a book titled "Karezza. Ethics of Marriage".[6] A German translation appeared already one year later. The translator, a certain Dr. Hartung, general practitioner in Silesia, praised Stockham as a "soul-curing physician of mankind authorized by her science".[7] In his preface he just stressed Stockham's principles of healing and nutrition without mentioning her natural philosophical and religious ideas. The well-known

---

[6] Alice Bunker Stockham: Karezza. Ethics of Marriage. Chicago: A. B. Stockham & co., 1896.
[7] Alice Bunker Stockham: Die Reform-Ehe. Ein Mittel zur Erhöhung der Daseinsfreude und zur Veredelung des Menschengeschlechts. Autorisirte deutsche Uebersetzung von H. B. Fischer. Vorrede: Dr. Hartung. Hagen i.W.: Risel, 1897, pp. VII-XI.

Swiss life reformer and naturist Werner Zimmermann translated the second edition (Chicago 1903) – which is reprinted here – almost 30 years after the first one published in 1896.[8]

Stockham was convinced, that there was a tremendous difference between the usual copulation and the Karezza conjunction or merging. She opposed them fundamentally as the following quotations show: "The ordinary hasty spasmodic method of cohabitation, for which there has been no previous preparation, and in which the wife is passive is alike unsatisfactory to husband and wife. It is deleterious both physically and spiritually. It has in it no consistency as a demonstration of affection, and is frequently a cause of estrangement and separation".[9] In contrast the Karezza merging would be satisfactory, healthy, and heaven on earth: "During a lengthy period of perfect control, the whole being of each is merged into the other, and an exquisite exaltation experienced. This may be accompanied by a quiet motion, entirely under subordination of the will, so that the thrill of passion for either may not go beyond a pleasurable exchange. [...], with abundant time and mutual reciprocity the interchange becomes satisfactory and complete without emission [i.e. ejaculation] or crises. In the course of an hour the physical tension subsides, the spiritual exaltation increases, and not uncommonly visions of a transcendent life are seen and consciousness of new powers experienced."[10]

Stockham's concept of Karezza never became popular, neither in academia nor in everyday life. There were a very few celebrities appreciating her ideas. We should mention at the first place the Russian writer Leo Tolstoy as already noted. Another authority being open-minded to Karezza was the English sexologist Havelock Ellis, who corresponded also with Sigmund Freud on the problem of sexuality and anticipated the concept of auto-erotism and narcissism. Freud cited him often, espe-

---

[8] Alice Bunker Stockham: Ethik der Ehe. Karezza. Berechtigte Übersetzung aus dem Amerikanischen von Werner Zimmermann. Jena; Bern: Die Neue Zeit, 1925.
[9] See Chapter II.
[10] See Chapter II.

cially in his "Interpretation of Dreams". It is remarkable but not astonishing, that Freud himself did not take any notice of Stockham, who did not belong to the scientific community. But even more astonishing is the fact, that sexology (*Sexualwissenschaft*) and sexual medicine (*Sexualmedizin*) enfolding in the early 20th century especially in Germany and also the scientific debate following the so-called sexual revolution of the 1960s ignored Karezza almost completely. Even the recent feminist movement and the corresponding gender debate forgot about Stockham.

In general, her work seemed to be suspicious, either for biological reasons as an inappropriate method of sexual satisfaction or for moral reasons as an unnatural method contradicting divine laws. The most prominent opponent for moral reasons was the papal authority. Forty years after her death in 1912, Pope Pius XII. rejected a so-called "reserved embrace" referring indirectly to Karezza, which was forbidden for priests and spiritual directors to recommend. In his "allocution to midwives" in 1951 he cited Pope Pius XI's Encyclical *Casti Connubii* (chaste wedlock) in 1930: "...that every attempt of either husband or wife in the performance of the conjugal act or in the development of its natural consequences which aims at depriving it of its inherent force and hinders the procreation of new life is immoral and that no 'indication' of need can convert an act which is intrinsically immoral into a moral and lawful one. / The precept is in full force today, as it was in the past, and so it will be in the future also, and always, because it is not a simple human whim, but the expression of a natural and divine law."[11]

I think it's worthwhile to remember Alice B. Stockham, an outstanding doctor and philanthropist, who practised in a humanistic manner in Chicago fighting for a better life and who died here about 100 years ago. Apart from her published writings I could not detect any archival material like correspondences or manuscripts in the United States or elsewhere.[12] I was officially told, that nothing is left in any US repository.

---

[11] http://en.wikipedia.org/wiki/Alice_Bunker_Stockham#cite_note-5 (April, 25, 2017)
[12] Please, contact the editor, if you know anything about up to now unknown material.

Nevertheless, it is remarkable, that in certain esoteric circles her book on Karezza is still on sale. It is time, that the scientific community recognizes her important idea of a spiritual or mental emancipation from sexual bestiality. In my opinion, Stockham is a fascinating figure for medical and cultural historiography in the overlapping fields of natural philosophy and religious thinking, mesmerism and psychoanalysis, medical anthropology and sexology, feminism and social hygiene, and last but not least humanism and pacifism. It is time to rediscover her life and work.

*****

***

KAREZZA

ETHICS OF MARRIAGE

BY

ALICE B. STOCKHAM, M. D.

AUTHOR OF TOKOLOGY, KORADINE,
HEALTH GERMS, ETC.

Honor to womanhood and reverence for maternity, are conditions of per
manency in any people, nation or race.—*Farnham*.

NEW EDITION

CHICAGO
STOCKHAM PUBLISHING CO.